Your Happiness
Might Only Be Medium

Your Happiness
Might Only Be Medium

Some Original Epigrammatic Poems
- Large Print Version

Martin Wasserman

To order additional copies of this book, contact:
Xlibris
844-714-8691
www.Xlibris.com
Orders@Xlibris.com

A Word from the Author

An epigrammatic poem is a short, pithy piece of verse which, through humor, or by making a blatant statement, expresses a single thought or observation. I mention this almost universally accepted definition for the epigram because there is one major difference between an epigrammatic poem written in German and one that is composed in English. The standard for any piece of good poetry in English, including the lyrical epigram, is that the words and lines flow in some type of metrical pattern, whether that pattern be iambic pentameter, iambic tetrameter or, for that matter, any other kind of established metrical form. However, when epigrammatic verse is written in German, the criterion strived for is not that of being metrical but, rather, how close a piece of verse can come to sounding like ordinary speech or conversation. Walter Kaufmann, the eminent translator and essayist, has stressed this fact. He bluntly states that when it comes to doing translation work on epigrammatic poems, those persons "who consider it their job to transpose all they touch into whatever they consider poetic or the peculiar verse idiom of the day miss the point that most German epigrammatists have always tried to stay extremely close to the spoken language."

In my current project I took Kaufmann's observation one step further and used the German model to write my original English epigrammatic poems. In other words, I chose to write my original poems in a way that would sound very much like everyday spoken English. I envisioned, with each piece I was working on, that the poem itself actually represented a particular set of verbal remarks that I wished to personally convey to the reader. The reader, hopefully, would then be thrust into the dual roles of both reader and listener; and this desirable situation could next set the stage for initiating a strong "writer-reader-listener" connection which of course was my goal all along.

New York 2021   Martin Wasserman

YOUR HAPPINESS MIGHT ONLY BE MEDIUM

Children
       are surely philosophers—
after all,
       they wonder and doubt
day after day.

—

A life
    filled with objects
that actually work—
    surely a source of great comfort.

—

The most precious time
in all eternity—
it's this very moment!

—

A frigid January night—
even snow buntings
don't wish
to greet
the next morning.

—

The orchid thrives
    though often outnumbered
by thorns and thistles.

——

New thought,
    deep thought,
best thought.

—

Time can cure, console,
even beautify
a wearisome life.

—

Change
    is miraculous
only when all have changed.

—

Misfortune,
    itself,
is unable to stop
    a life
of pure determination.

—

Each problem
    has within it
a special gem
    for those who search
with great depth.

—

Here's what a closer look
     can reveal—
some lessons
     on shifting perceptions.

—

The choice
   of not making a choice
can often be
   the wisest choice.

—

Violence
    in the name of strength
is merely weakness
disguised as a virtue.

—

Recognizing the madness
    within oneself;
can it be
    a first step
towards personal enlightenment?

—

Provincialism,
	prejudice, pride—
beware of these three traits.

—

For those who possess great confidence—
save some for yourself
but give the rest away.

—

Springtime—
    the butterfly questions
but only the bee
    will answer.

—

To clear your mind,
listen
to the melody
of streams.

—

The nucleus of a snowflake
   is tiny
but attracts
   volumes of snow
all around it.

—

How courageous it is
to see oneself
strictly through the eyes
of the "other."

—

A struggle for equality
is the bare necessity
for reaching equality.

—

Wherever you find yourself,
dreams of the sea
can invigorate your soul.

—

Commitment,

compassion,

cooperation—

make these your lifelong virtues.

—

Still celebrating
    prescribed holidays?
Your happiness
    might only be medium.

—

Philosophy
    would die a slow death
without the halo
    of poetry.

—

Liquor inebriates,
	coffee stimulates;
it's only tea that can soothe.

—

It's better
to live your life
like a free-flowing stream
than a stale, static pond.

—

Staying absolutely still—
it's quite
an adventure!

—

An ideal class—
    the students are joyous
despite
    being surrounded
by all the noise of the world.

—

Expansion, elation,
ecstasy—
a perplexing path
for those
who require tranquility.

—

One-to-one
conversations
often save the day.

—

Seawater can be enchanting,
even if beachcombers
see only sand.

—

What is the "sacred"?
It's the illumination of mystery
seen through a veiled
cosmic background.

—

Reorient, recreate, reinforce

until

hope and life are one.

—

One possible meaning of Zen—
"take a good rest
when you're tired."

—

Education requires
deep patience
on the part of those
being educated.

—

Bread, cheese, chocolate—
a good start
to making your peace
with others.

—

Meditating beneath the stars—
no need
for hills and streams.

—

Has the hoot owl
    truly sung
its nightly song
    if no one's there
to listen?

—

To destroy
is within us;
to heal,
also within us.

—

Ten below!
    A frozen lake,
dead grass,
    oak trees
bare and silent.

—

Aristotle pondered,

Gandhi meditated,

but today

machines do most of our thinking.

—

The secret to a good life—
don't grow older,
just newer.

—

Dark mountains
    leaning against the sky
often look
    like they're about to soar.

—

Compassion
can be
our tastiest food,
but only
if we're receptive
to its taste.

—

Human beings
    could learn a lot
from hummingbirds
    who always know
what's behind them.

—

What kills kindness?
    Certainly
wars of any kind;
    narrow-mindedness
will do it too.

—

9 781669 879305